SELF-PUBLISHING
101
for ANY1

Judith Falloon-Reid

Published by Independent VoYces Literary Works
Other books by Judith Falloon-Reid

- Sing Oral Sing
- The Smelly Seals of La Jolla (The Sleepy Adventures of Philomena Feinman series) Aaah-Inspiring Antarctica
- Antarctica Adventures with a Jamaican on Ice
- The Silent Stones
- Are Mirrors Cleaner in Paradise?
- Here's a Hundred Dollars…Buy Yourself a Life!
- Monday Morning Meditations
- Full Circle…Reclaiming Your Faith
- Time & Seasons. A Layman's Guide to Overcoming Tragedy

For more information and to order copies visit www.
jfalloon-reid.com

A Quick Word from the Author

Having self-published eleven books, including children's books, picture books and a manual or two, I consider myself somewhat knowledgeable in the field of self-publishing. This manual is a quick guide to help you prepare, print and market your self-published books.

Self-publishing is an option taken by many writers whose manuscripts have been rejected by traditional publishers. Traditional publishers have their own individual lists of elements that they look for when deciding whether or not to accept a manuscript, not least of which is a personal connection with the manuscript presented to them. Basically, if the publisher doesn't like it or doesn't think it will sell, the book will be rejected. They receive thousands of submissions annually and publish less than 10% of those submissions. If you are rejected, you are not alone. Vanity publishers, though paid by authors, can sometimes refuse to publish your work if it doesn't meet their own standards.

Rejection is not an indictment on the writer. It is, in fact, worth getting. So if you believe you have a winner, you should submit your manuscript to traditional publishers. If you are rejected make note of their comments so you can use them, where relevant, to better your book.

Self-publishing is not for the easily discouraged. It takes work, money, time, more time and serious commitment to success.

Judith Falloon-Reic

The who, what, when, where & how...

Gone are the days when a writer had to submit his or her manuscript to a publisher only to be ignored or instantly turned down and left with the impression that his or her book will never be published.

Today, self-published books are commonplace. They offer the opportunity for you as a writer to:

1. **Express** your own thoughts in your own ways
2. Have **complete ownership** and control of your work, design, time lines, quantities and distribution.
3. **Determine the scope of your work** without word count and page constraints imposed by traditional publishers.
4. Have **flexibility** of time and lower printing costs afforded by print-on-demand technology
5. Keep **more money** per copy in your own pocket
6. Publish **special interest books** such as how-to guides and single events
7. Publish materials of local or regional interest at **relatively low cost**

That said, it's time to examine the who, what, when, where and how of self-publishing.

Motives & Goals

Why are you publishing?

Contrary to the belief of many traditional publishers, not all authors write to become famous or rich from their work. There are many different motivations - some of which work well for the argument of self-publishing.

Here are a few common reasons for publishing:

- To become famous and a best-selling author
- To share your work with your family, friends and community
- For posterity
- Because you feel you have something valuable to contribute to a particular affinity group
- Everyone has told you how good a writer you are and you should publish
- To see the fulfillment of a dream
- As a tool to be used in workshops and seminars
- To attract the attention of a traditional publisher
- To document an experience that can only be expressed in pictures or words

Set yourself goals.

What are your GOALS

Some examples are:
- Publication date
- The number of books you want to sell
- A print deadline
- Appearing as a talk show guest
- Who is your target audience

Now think about your own motives and goals. Write them down. That will make them more real to you. What is your motivation? What are your goals? Write down as many as come to mind.

How do YOU define success?

Here are some sobering statistics before you decide how to define success.

- The average book published in the U.S. sells fewer than 2,000 copies in its lifetime.
- The average self-published book sells 200 – 500 copies in its lifetime
- A small percentage of bestselling authors self-published their own work prior to being picked up by a taditional publisher.

Now that we have got that out of the way, let me help you define success.

Define YOUR success by your OWN standards and YOUR OWN motives for publishing YOUR work. If what you want is to share your thoughts with as many people as possible then success is exactly that – sharing with as many as poss ble. That number can vary from 10 - 20,000 depending how you distribute your book.

Define success by how many books you sell. Set yourself a goal and work towarcs it, making check marks as you go along. Be realistic but don't be afraid to dream. If you put in the hard work it will pay off.

Define success by the lives you touch. If your book is inspirational or self-help, you can choose to define yourself by the people who have been touched or have had their lives changed by your words.

Define success by digging in your heels and going the whole distance. Books never die. Revamp, refresh and rebirth your old books as new.

How do you define your success?

There are many steps to be taken before you are ready to publish your book.

Get you manuscript ready!

This may seem like an obvious statement, after all, you can't publish a book you haven't written. Yet writing is just the beginning.

Step 1. Write the book. Read the book. Rewrite the book. Re-read the book.

Repeat this step as often as needed until you feel your book is ready for your trusted inner circle to read and give comments.

Step 2. Get feedback.

Send your manuscript to your inner circle and at least one writer you can trust. Ask for honest, constructive feedback. Be ready for open dialogue. This is important to:

- refining your story, poems or whatever materials lies within your pages
- ensuring your voice is clear and your message is understood
- gauging how others may perceive your book

Step 3. Decide how to use the feedback you have received. Be honest with and true to yourself.

Step 4. Make changes. You get to decide on the changes you want to make to your manuscript. Now is the time to make those changes before you send it to be edited.

Step 5. Get an editor!

Step 5. Get a proofreader!

Step 6. Design your book. Inner pages and cover.

Step 7: GET A PROOF COPY!
Always, always, get a proof copy before doing your final print run. This is your last chance to make minor changes and fix issues.

Step 8: Ta-daaa! Time to publish your book.

(Yes, you're seeing it right! Or did you miss it? There are Step 5 appears twice. This is why you need a proofreader!)

DON'T RUSH THE PROCESS!
MISTAKES HAPPEN WHEN YOU RUSH!

You NEED an Editor!

Your best friend is not necessarily the best judge of your writing (neither is your mom).
Get professional help!

You may have a great book in the making and your best friend may be telling you the truth about your writing, but don't rely solely on their judgement. The opinions of your friends and family DO count, however, as they help you to have an idea of a typical reader's response to your writing.

Have a professional copy editor work on your book to ensure that the thoughts you are conveying are well expressed and not just understood by you and those who know you. Your family and friends already understand how you think and speak therefore they will automatically read your manuscript with that in mind. A good editor makes your work better.

It is important that the editor you choose has experience editing the genre of work you have written.

Some factors a copy editor will take into consideration include:
- Your audience
- Your market
- Syntax, sentence construction, punctuation
- Clarity of thought
- Continuity, chronology & logic
- Your writing style and tone
- The genre of the book

Where do you find an editor?

Ask around, look online, ask an author who has a book similar to yours in genre and length. Don't be shy about interviewing and author and discuss your personal writing style and idiosyncrasies with the eidtor before they begin working on your manuscript. The more the editor knows about you and your work, the better the outcome.

Getting your manuscript fully ready BEFORE designing saves time and money!

Your English teacher is not a proofreader
Get professional help!

Your manuscript should meet the same standards as traditionally published books with which you are competing for readership.

Your English teacher may catch all your grammar mistakes and spell check may catch some spelling mistakes, but who is going to catch the errors in chronology? Or the fact that your character's name changed from Anne to Annie? Who will help you organize the book so it makes for better reading? Who will do your fact check?

Professional copyediting and proofreading are essential to producing a good book and these two functions should not be done by the same person.

Books differ in how much editing they need. The minimum is two rounds of editing in addition to two rounds of proofreading. Most need more but it's well worth the money spent. The last thing you want is someone reviewing your book and commenting on how much better it would have been if there weren't so many errors! Perfect may be unattainable but strive to come as close as possible.

Proof read this:
The seamen accomplished a great feat by hoisting there catch of four million pounds of fish from the chilling waters of the Pacific unto the deck of the rolling fishing vessel.
It was no mean feet by any stretch of the imagination

that they wore able to carry out this task. The taskmaster shouted loudly to the reporter" I wish I could have seen them create such grate history. It was a colorful event."

Make a note of the things you think your computer or friend may have missed.

Corrections:

Designing your book

Designing your book is more than selecting a cover image.
It is ensuring the following:
- Page layout is consistent and enhances the reading experience
- Images are the right size and orientation
- Appropriate software is used
- Files are saved and output correctly
- Colours are true based on the output you require and not your monitor

Hiring a designer
If you are not creatively inclined and have the funds to hire a designer, this is your best option for producing a book that meets all the specs and design elements for a professionally produced book. Using an experienced designer saves time and minimizes mistakes.
Be sure to ask if the designer has experience designing books and ask for samples.

Where to find a designer?
- Ask for references
- Fiverr is affordable
- Your publisher can help (if you're using a publisher)

But even if you are working with a designer, if you have a very tight budget, there is a lot you can do for yourself such as:
- **Prepare your manuscript and deliver it already edited and proofread**
- Select and purchase your own cover image(s)
- Layout your manuscript in a format that makes it easily

transferable to the design program (a word doc without formatting)
- Select your own colour palette
- Conceptualize your own cover design

Take note:
Microsoft Word is a word processing program. IT IS NOT A DESIGN PROGRAM. It may have the capacity to perform many of your layout functions but it is not a graphics programme and it does not work well with images.

If you are hiring a designer, ask the designer how they would like to receive the manuscript. If doing it yourself, Google is your friend. Information abounds. YouTube is your friend. Tutorials abound.

Your Book Cover

Your book cover should reflect your title and look just as eye-catching, professional and compelling as that of a book published by a vanity or traditional publisher. Take your time in selecting your cover image and designing your book cover. Unless you are a designer or have lots of time and ink on your hands, you may need to have a professional designer assist with designing your cover.

Selecting your cover image

Option 1
Most printers will offer book cover design services which include selecting an image they feel is most appropriate for your book title. Usually they will get it right.

Option 2
Don't overlook your own feelings about what you want your book cover to look and feel like. There are numerous stock photography houses from which you can purchase the rights to use an image, some for as little as US$15. If you wish to choose your own image, take the time to search for the right image.

Option 3
Select your own image and send it to the printer for them to use in designing your book.

Below are three popular stock image websites that offer affordable choices:
www.istock.com
www.shutterstock.com
www.bigstockimages.com
For more expensive, exclusive options try:
www.gettyimages.com
www.corbisimages.com

Option 4
Embrace AI

Design templates vs. custom design
Many book cover designers use cover templates. Templates can vary greatly so take your time to choose one that reflects the intended look and feel of your book and the emotions you are trying to convey to your audience.

If your book is one of a series, you may need a design template to ensure that the next book in the series is instantly recognizable.

Custom designs are perfect and worth the extra money if you want a unique cover that only you could have thought of or if you want your book to have an effect that only you or the designer can convey.

Remember the spine!

The spine of your book is just as important as the cover of your book. If your book cannot be identified when it's sitting sideways on a shelf, no-one will know it's there!

Your back cover
Decide what information you want on your back cover such as:
- A summary of your book
- Recommendations or quotations from noteworthy persons and or media houses
- Your image and bio are good if it's for a local readership. Rethink this for the international market if you are virtually unknown. It can prejudice your book with booksellers and readers in some markets. It can also stereotype your book before it's read.
- Consider two versions of your cover depending on your market

Designing the interior pages
Organizing the inside of your book: Paragraphs, fonts, headlines, sizes, et al

Whether your book is being printed by a traditional printer or a print on demand printer, you can usually get help in deciding on the interior style of your book. But before you get to that point, spend some time in bookstores looking through a wide variety of books. Make a note of the style elements that grab your attention. If you are laying out your book yourself or having it laid out by someone you know, your options are greater. Here are some points to consider when organizing your book.

Chapters
- New chapters sometimes start a half, third or quarter way down the new page
- Some books use a symbol or graphic below or above new chapter headings.
- Chapters can be named or just have numbers.
- Decide whether to use all caps, initial caps or a variation of both.
- Does it matter if a chapter starts on a left page or do you prefer them all starting on right page? This will affect your page count and remember that your page count increases your printing price.

Fonts
If your audience is likely to be middle aged to more mature, medium to large fonts may be best.
- For interior pages block fonts are always better than script fonts.
- Fancy fonts with curves and loops may look good in your title but should not be used in the body of your work. Make sure your fancy font is readable.
- Remember some fonts don't translate "&" and other symbols and others won't offer you the options for bold or italics.

Fonts can convey their own feelings by their shape and style.

Business fonts: Arial ,Times New Roman, Garamond
Playful fonts: Happy Sans, Curlz MT, Playbill
Stylish fonts: Vivaldi, EdwardianScript,Monotype Corsiva
Scary fonts: chiller,Juice ITC
Fonts for limited space: Arial Narrow,Agency FB, Gill Sans
Condensed

Paragraphs
- Should your first paragraph be indented or not?
- Decide whether to use a single space or preset space between paragraphs.
- Justified text looks neater and presents a cleaner page.
- Margins are important to the reading experience.
- Control word wraps, orphans and widows. An orphan is a word that appears by itself at the beginning of a page or the beginning of a line. A widow is the last line of a paragraph that appears at the top of a page.
- Be aware of the length of paragraphs. Paragraphs that are too long can affect the reading experience.

Headers & Footers
- Decide on how you want the headers and footers to appear in your book, for example, the book title and author's name on alternate pages in the header.
- Select your preferred format for your page numbers. Do you prefer simply using a number or a number along with the word "page"?
- Do you want your page numbers centered or off to the side.

Book size
Some deciding factors:
- What feels good and right in your hands and how

will that be affected by the number of pages in your manuscript.

- The type of book you have written; whether it's a novel, cook book, pictorial, etc.

Compare book types and sizes and make note of what other writers have used for similar books. Their choice may or may not work for your book.

Remember, the more work your layout team does is the more it will likely cost. Simple is sometimes best. Knowing what you want before you order minimizes costs.

Let's talk about Online DIY resources!

There are a myriad of online graphics apps, programs and resources you can use to design your book covers and help to format your book. Below I mention two of the most common ones.

- Easy to use
- Access to images, graphics, AI tools
- Basic image editing tools
- Catalogue of fonts
- Allows collaboration
- Affordable upgraded version

Let's talk about KDP covers!

Kindle Publishing Direct
We will talk more about KDP later on, but did you know that KDP has a cover creator within its publishing set up? When you upload a manuscript, KDP has an option for you to create a cover within the setup.

Outsourcing your design
In addition to using a designer in person, there are affordable design services available online from gig-economy sources such as Fiverr.com. Go exploring!

The Question
of Artificial
Intelligence

Whether to use AI or not is a personal decision. From designing your book cover to helping you write to designing the interior, there is an app for that.

Firstly let's look at how AI works.
AI creates using prompts that sends it in search of what already exists from which it then creates.

Advantages:
- Quick, easy way to create
- Generates ideas you can use
- Generates diverse options
- Insight into market trends
- Affordability
- Professional outcomes for a fraction of the price

Disadvantages
- Lack of creativity and originality
- Technical issues and distorted images
- Inconsistencies possible with design
- Quality not always hi-res
- Lacks human emotion and subject understanding

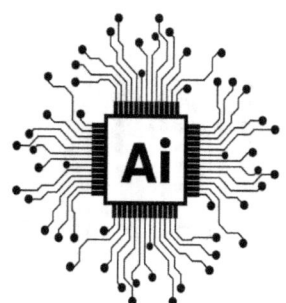

Designing with AI

AI can offer a quick, easy, cost effective way to create your book cover. There are more AI programs to choose from than you will ever need so go exploring!

Things to consider when using AI as your designer:

1. The intelligence is artificial. AI cannot think nor create for itself. This means you need to input the correct prompts to get the results you desire. You may need to tweak and revise your prompts many times before receiving your desired output.

2. Duplicating a result is not guaranteed. The image created by a prompt may change the next time you input the same prompt.

3. Your result may not be unique. Because AI pulls its intelligence from already existing data, your design may not be unique to you if someone else inputs the same prompts.

4. AI can adversely affect the creativity that comes from human talent

How do you feel about using AI to design your book?

Printing your book
All printers are not created equally

Not all printers are experts at printing books. Printers are not publishers and publishers are not printers. Know the difference.

Choosing a printer

Choosing the right printer for your book will determine how much preparation of your manuscript is necessary and is crucial to the final outcome. Let's start by looking at the two options and how these will affect your workload.

Traditional printing

Several local printers are experienced with printing books. They offer personalized, face-to-face service and because they are local, you will not need to worry about shipping or delivery costs for your book. If you choose a traditional overseas printer, be sure to ask for a sample of their work before agreeing to use their services.

Traditional printers have established minimum print runs and your cost will depend on the quantity of books you are printing at any given time. For a writer with limited resources, this can mean a substantial investment of funds and stocking many more books than you may need initially.

Print on Demand (POD)

Unless you feel an absolute need to meet with your printer face-to-face, or you have the money to pay a printer to print a large quantity of books in one print run, online printing offers the fastest, most economical way to print your self-published book.

POD technology makes it easy for writers to print small quantities of books as needed. Traditional printers demand that a large quantity of books be printed at any one time to realize any savings. All online, self-publishing printers use print-on-demand technology.

How does POD work?

POD technology stores your book digitally so that the book can be printed as needed on high speed, efficient digital presses. Depending on the printer you choose, your book price will either vary with the quantity or will remain constant regardless of how many you print. POD technology can print as few as 1 book and as many as thousands as ordered.

Most POD printers have packages for you to choose from; some with bells and whistles that will be discussed later on in this guide book. Some offer their own online bookstores where your books can be sold and orders fulfilled in real time without you having to stock books.

Do your research and compare prices and services before making a decision. **KDP is a good choice for individual cost and speed.**

Is there a set up charge as well as per book fees? Charges vary from printer to printer and are also based on what is required.

Printing when using a vanity publisher is different.

As mentioned before, vanity publishers charge fees to publish your book. In reality, you may still be considered self-published because you paid someone to publish and handle all the entire process, but it is still your work your way. You still have a say in what is printed.

Some vanity publishers charge a set-up fee which includes your book layout, cover design, spine design, choice of fonts and paragraph layout plus a per book charge which remains constant regardless of quantity. Some specialize in niche markets but still offer a variety of services.

But if you are capable of laying out your own book and designing your own covers, or have someone doing it for you so that your file is print ready, then all you need is a printer. Traditional or POD? Local or Overseas such as China? Do your research!

ALWAYS Print a galley!

Regardless of how you choose to publish or who is printing your book, ALWAYS print a galley.

A galley is a proof copy of your book printed and temporarily bound exactly as the final copy is expected to be printed and bound. Even if you get your files from your printer digitally, it is worth it to spend the extra money to ensure that your pages fall where you want them to fall, the alignment of chapters is correct, and all your elements are in good order.

If you are using a print on-demand service, have them print and send you one copy of the book prior to ordering the larger amounts. If you make changes to an issue, be sure to print out the new version.

There is nothing worse than spending lots of money to order copies of a book that is anything but correctly printed and bound.

**SLOW DOWN! PLAN AHEAD!
DON'T RUSH THE PROCESS!**

Copyrighting Your Work

Your copyright is implicit in your published work. There is no need to apply for a copyright but it is a good idea to do so. Whether you do or not, however, you need to protect that right.

Register your copyright formally at the appropriate copyright office based on where you live. A simple online search can help you to find that information.

Poor man's copyright
Mail a sealed copy of your work to yourself. Upon receiving it DO NOT OPEN THE PACKAGE. Keep it, unopened, in a safe place. f ever there is an issue with someone else claiming rights to your work, the unopened mailed copy can be used in court to prove your ownership. Unless the other party has proof that he/she wrote the work prior to the date stamp on your package, your copyright cannot be challenged.

Email your work to yourself and every version thereof. Create a folder and keep those emails.

Your copyright page
Your book should have a title page which is the first thing your reader sees once they open the cover. The title page helps to identify your book should the cover get damaged or inadvertently removed.

Following your title page, most frequently on the reverse side is your copyright page. This page is important and necessary to establish your copyright, identify the book edition, publication date(s), publisher and other publication details. Your copy editor will help you with this.

Copyright pages are fairly standard so feel free to copy the format for your copyright page from any copy of a published book.

Protecting your copyright
Join a collective agency now. Before, during or after you publish you should join a collective agency.
As a Jamaican author, I will use my Jamaican experience here as an example. JAMCOPY (Jamaican Copyright Licensing Agency) is the organization to which I belong. There is no membership fee.

JAMCOPY, the Jamaican Copyright Licensing Agency, is a collective management organization and Jamaica's national Reproduction Rights Organization (RRO). It was set up by creators and publishers of materials published in printed form, to manage their reproduction rights. The Jamaica Copyright Act 1993 gives all creators sole and exclusive right to publish and reproduce their work in any form (www.jamcopy.com.)

Research the RRO that manages rights in your territory and become a member.

Getting that mysterious ISBN International Standard Book Number

If you plan to sell your book or have it recognized internationally then you must get an ISBN. Each ISBN is unique to an edition of a book and identifies the publisher of the book. Your e-book version needs a different ISBN than your audio book version and your printed book version of the same title.

You need to have this number ready before you print your book. On demand publishers can also provide you with an ISBN number, usually included in their set up fee. This number, however, identifies them as the publisher and not you. If you publish with KDP (Amazon's online publishing platform), you can get a free ISBN when you upload your manuscript.

An ISBN can be bought individually or in batches. If you plan to publish several titles or different versions of the same title, it is far more economical to purchase in bulk. You can purchase these online or if you're in Jamaica, you can obtain your ISBN from the National Library of Jamaica. You can complete the registration, request and pay for your ISBN on their website. A quick phone call will answer all your questions.

Your book may be worth more (or less) to the reader than you think!

Pricing Your Book Books are usually priced by the number of pages. Traditionally, your publisher will set the price of your book. On demand printers will usually guide you with a suggested price for your book, also based on the number of pages.

As a self-published author, however, only you get to decide the price of your book.

So how do I price my book?

There are a number of factors to consider the first but not least of which is how much you are paying per copy to publish the book.

Remember to factor in:

- The per copy cost to print, including professional fees
- Delivery and/or shipping cost per copy shipped
- Number of pages and what other books with a similar number of pages in a similar genre are selling for
- The amount of profit you want to make per copy (30-50%)
- How much a bookstore will charge to sell your book (25 - 40%)
- YOUR time and effort
- The value of your name and goodwill. Are you a popular, known personality or totally unknown? Famous people will naturally command an audience, eager to buy their book.

- Where it will be sold: local, regional, international, online
- Cost of delivery to your reader such as shipping if applicable
- Customs duty if printed overseas (approx. 25% incl. all taxes) and broker's fees
- What your market can bear comfortably

The beauty of self-publishing is the ability to change the price of your book if it becomes necessary. You can do special promotions to jump start or encourage sales when they lag.

Pre-released books & "seconds"
There is always a chance that your first print run may have errors or you may spot a few minor changes you'd like to make. These books are not spoiled or useless. Sell them as pre-released or seconds for a lower cost than the final sale price of the book.

Direct prices vs. store prices
You may wish to offer a special price for books bought directly from you if you are doing private readings or if they are available on your website. Be careful, however, not to overtly undercut your local bookstore.

Marketing Your Masterpiece

So you've published the book. Yippee!
This is not the time to breathe. On the contrary, your work has just begun.

Be prepared to put 10 times more work into marketing, promoting and selling your book than you did into writing the book.

Begin before your book is printed. The marketing success or failure of your book will depend on how prepared you are before, during and after your book is printed.

Let's talk tools and how you can use all the tools available to build your toolbox and create a stellar marketing campaign?

Equip your tool box!
First things first! Create a marketing plan!

BEFORE
- **Press kit** – Prepare a press kit for your book. Include a choice of photos of yourself including a professional photo and your book cover, a well written biography, summary of the book and a press release. Create this in email format as well as print. Invest in an attractive digital media kit.

- **Press releases:** Get help with writing your press release. Don't forget local community events and newsletters.
- **Promotional copies** – Set aside promotional copies for bookstores, media and influential people who can help you promote your book. These copies can come from your pre-released copies or seconds. Mark them promotional copies – not to be sold.
- **Promotional materials** – Get them ready. Business cards, book markers and a variety of promotional items are available. Think of a few that are unique to you.
- **Online presence is a MUST**– Personal website, Facebook and other social media.
- **Set up merchant services** to take credit cards – You can do it yourself.
- **Research, research, research** – FREE Online resources for authors are readily available.

DURING
- While your book is being printed, **create a buzz!** Count down the days to release online using, for example, the Facebook page you created for your book. Get creative!
- Offer **special pre-released prices** to your friends if they order early.
- Use all forms of **social media** and use them often
- Take advantage of AI tools to **create reels, book trailers etc**

AFTER
- **Bookstore distribution**: knock on every door or find a distributor (be sure to have flyers and posters!)
- **Get a copy to the arts/book editor** for your local newspaper and every media you can find.

- **Amazon.com:** You can do it yourself. Visit kdp.amazon.com, open an account and follow the directions in the Kindle Publishing Guide.
- **Create your ebook**
- Research **book clubs and television shows** that promote books
- **Book parties, book readings and book signings** should never stop. Bring bookmarks, posters and other giveaways that relate to your book.
- **Offer yourself** as a public speaker.
- **Become an expert** in the subject matter of your book.
- **Donate books** to the local library and libraries abroad when you travel.
- **Enter writing contests.**
- **Stay in touch with the bookstores and your distributor.** Visit the stores where your books are being sold and look for your book on the shelf. Check placement.
- **Traditional media campaigns** are also useful.
- **Hire a publicist.** (if your budget can handle it.)
- Get a copy of your book to the **National Library of Jamaica** and talk to the **Jamaica Library service** about adding copies of your book to their collections.
- Employ **Guerrilla Marketing** tactics.
- **Network, network, network**
- **Think outside the box.** Just because it hasn't been done doesn't mean it can't be done!

ALWAYS HAVE A BOOK AND PROMOTIONAL CARDS WITH YOU!

What are some other innovative ideas for marketing your work?

_____

_____

_____

_____

_____

_____

_____

_____

_____

_____

Do's & Dont's of Self-Publishing

DO publish your work! No matter what anyone else says or thinks, seeing your words in a book gives a sense of great pride and accomplishment!

DO define your own motive for publishing and realize when that motive has been fulfilled. All else is gravy!

DO get professional help! Even if your book is for a select few, a badly written or laid out book is still a badly done piece of work. Take time to select your cover images and the interior design layout of your book. Take pride in your book.

DO block all negativity but accept constructive criticism of your work. Learn to accept constructive criticism with grace and dignity.

DO market aggressively to get the media, publishers, bookstores and others to notice your book, review it and stock it.

DO your research! Before selecting a printer/publisher, do your homework. Compare several and be sure you are comparing apples to apples.

DON'TS

DON'T underestimate your work or yourself. My brother who makes films once told me "if you put it on TV, someone will watch it." He was right! The same applies to a well written book.

DON'T listen to naysayers. Many have achieved more with less and less with more.

DON'T limit yourself to the people you know, the town you live in, the media contacts you have, the way it's been done before. Get outside the box.

DON'T assume that just because traditional publishers rejected you before means they will reject you again. If that is your first goal, pursue it with every book you write and even after you have self-published your book.

DON'T give into failure if your first publication doesn't sell hundreds or thousands of copies. Keep writing and keep publishing your work but seek to get better each time.

From the pen of
JUDITH FALLOON-REID

Judith is an author, poet, Spoken word artist and filmmaker. Born and raised in Jamaica, she has authored eleven novels, children's books and inspirational self-help books. *Aaah-Inspiring Antarctica*, a coffee table book and *Antarctica Adventures with a Jamaican on Ice*, a children's book, chronicle her journey as the first Jamaican woman to visit Antarctica. In 2020, she successfully staged an exhibition of her photos, film, and books at the National Library of Jamaica, where the exhibit remained for a month before going on an international tour which was interrupted by the pandemic.

She is the writer and director of four award-winning Faith-based movies, *70 x Seventy, Just Another Friday, The Gift Everlasting* and *Just Another Friday 2* and the television series, *Mirrors in Paradise* commissioned in 2023 by Public Broadcasting station PBCJ Jamaica. The series was filmed and produced by BarriVision Films, a production company she shares as equal partner with her husband Michael Brown. Her short films include, *iWitness, Aaah-Inspiring Antarctica - a Jamaican on Ice* and *A Deep Breath*.

The creator of several Caribbean television shows including *My Likkle Food Spot, Where in JA is Dry Lan' Touris?* and *Gospel Rhythms* as well as the host of *Shelf Life*, she has over 40 years' experience as a writer including as a newspaper columnist and travel writer.

Judith is a participant in the annual Jamaica Poets Nomadic School Tour which she helps to coordinate along with the tour's founder, Dub Poet Malachi Smith. She is also an annual workshop presenter, host and panelist at Caricon Literary conference in Los Angeles and in 2022 Judith was recognized by the City of Los Angeles for her life's work in the arts.

Her latest mission is rooted in developing the Travel 2 Educate program that seeks to educate youth across Jamaica especially, through film, photos, books and talks about her travels. Through this program, she hopes to expose them to the world beyond their shores while feeding their imaginations and elevating their consciousness. The Aaah-Inspiring Antarctica Experience was the pilot project for this program.

In 2022, Judith and Michael relocated to Panama though they travel frequently to Jamaica and worldwide for performances, workshops and film projects.

With God always at the center of her life, she is passionate about family, the creative arts, Missions and helping others achieve their goals.

For more information visit www.jfalloon-reid.com.

www.ingramcontent.com/pod-product-compliance
Lightning Source LLC
Chambersburg PA
CBHW070141230526
45472CB00004B/1636